AF483123

AMERICAN BATTLEFIELD

THE FIGHT FOR THE WHITE HOUSE

THOMAS PAINE JR

AMERICAN BATTLEFIELD

THOMAS PAINE JR

INTRODUCTION

My Fellow Americans! Brace yourselves for the gloomy update - the menacing Emperor Bidifer is up to no good!

Enemy troops, under the rule of Evil Emerita and The Shape Shiffter, have triumphed over all main cities in the US.

The mighty armed forces of the United States have been vanquished. The White House has been conquered!

After a nail-biting three-year battle, Lord Ackmith, Inaf, and Braggor emerged victorious! Emperor Bidifer could now claim the White House as his own. The booming voice of American patriotism fell silent at last.

Leaping into action, the notorious duo Evil Emerita and The Shape Shiffter, under Emperor Bidifer's command, have successfully captured President Trump and locked him up!
The American people were now utterly helpless, caught in a desperate situation, entirely under the thumb of Emperor Bidifer!

Emperor Bidifer's ambitions soared higher still. He captured every soul who had once raised the banner of Old Glory and cast them into the depths of captivity.

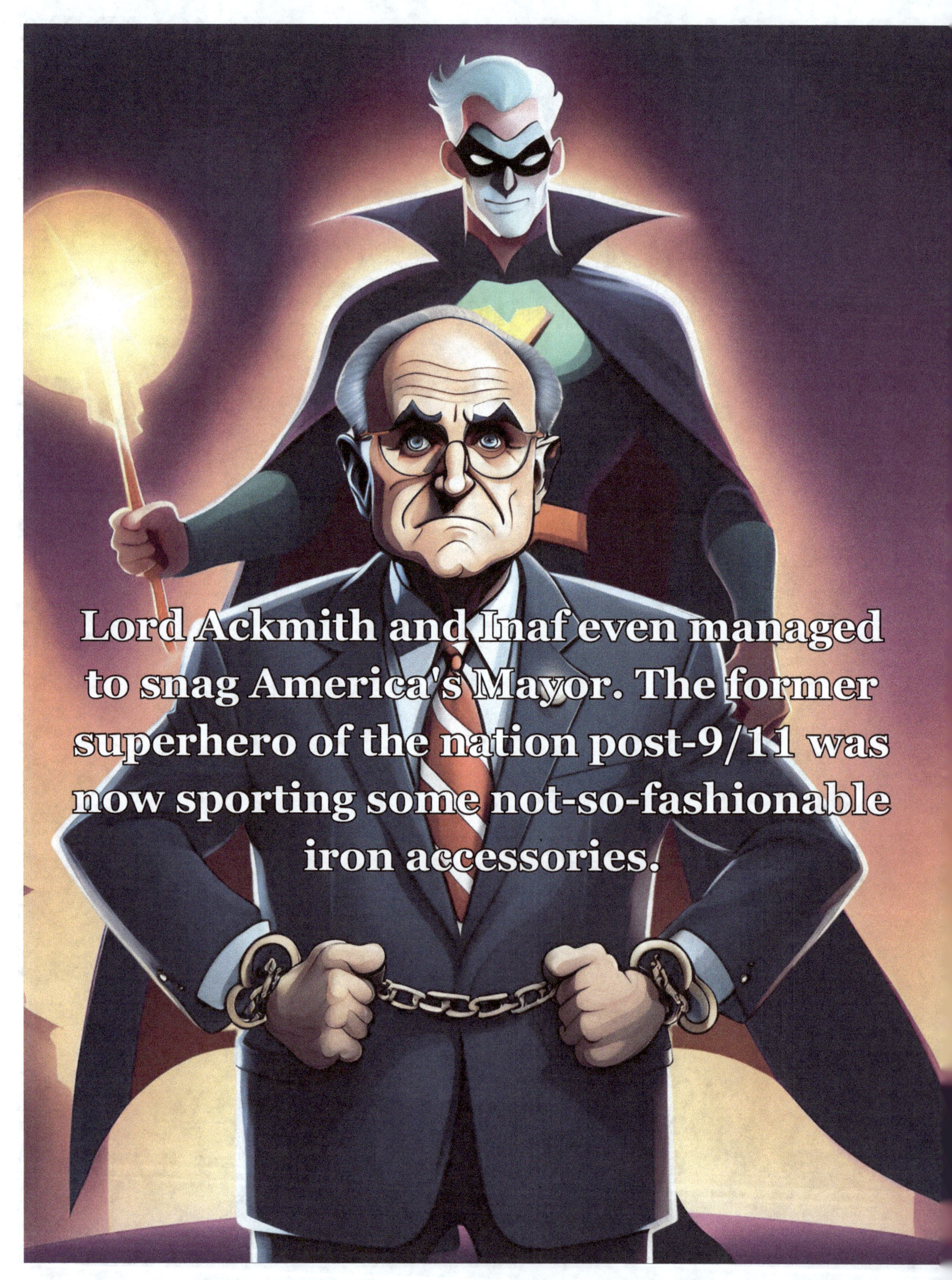
Lord Ackmith and Inaf even managed
to snag America's Mayor. The former
superhero of the nation post-9/11 was
now sporting some not-so-fashionable
iron accessories.

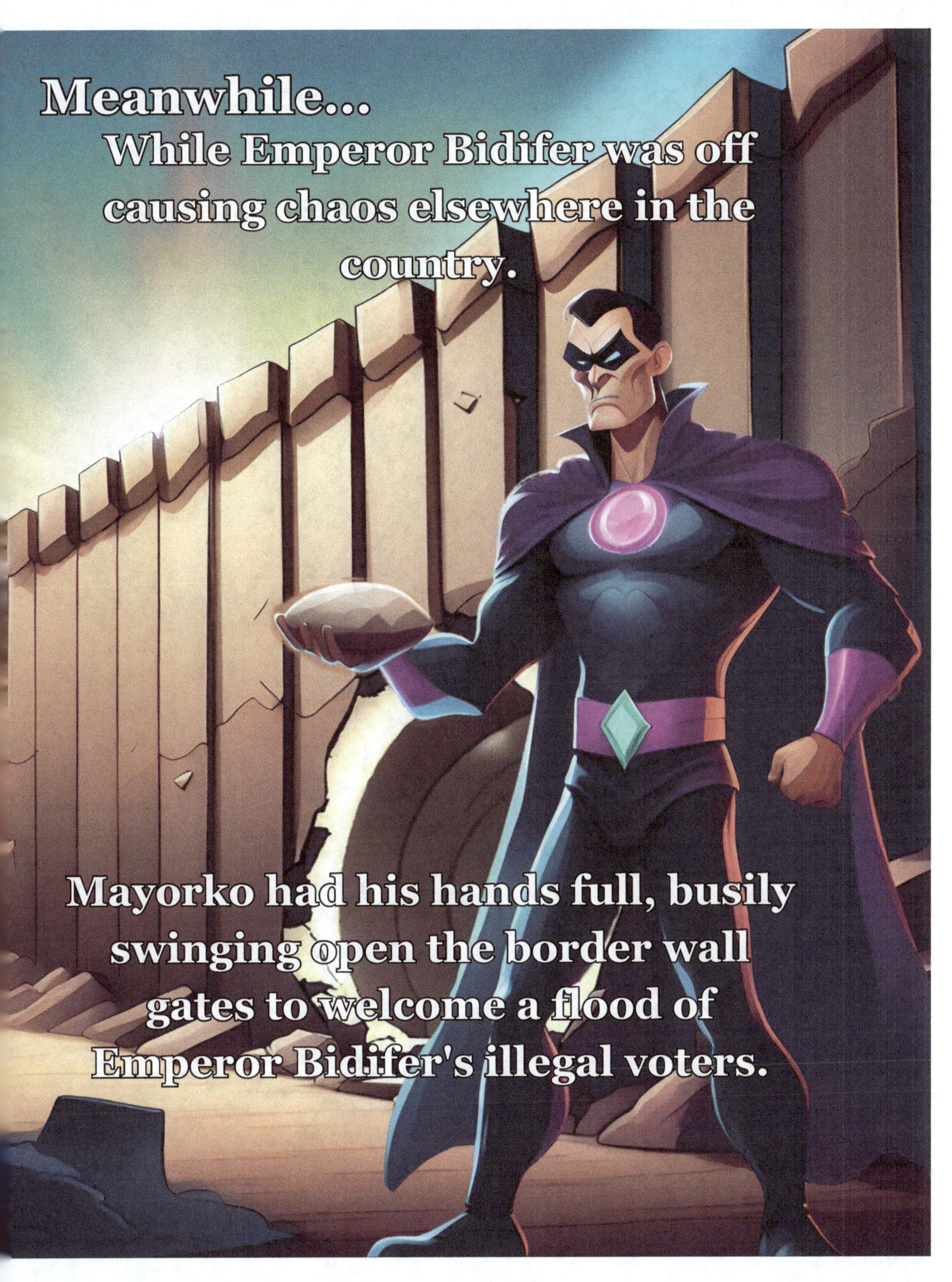

Meanwhile...
While Emperor Bidifer was off causing chaos elsewhere in the country.
Mayorko had his hands full, busily swinging open the border wall gates to welcome a flood of Emperor Bidifer's illegal voters.

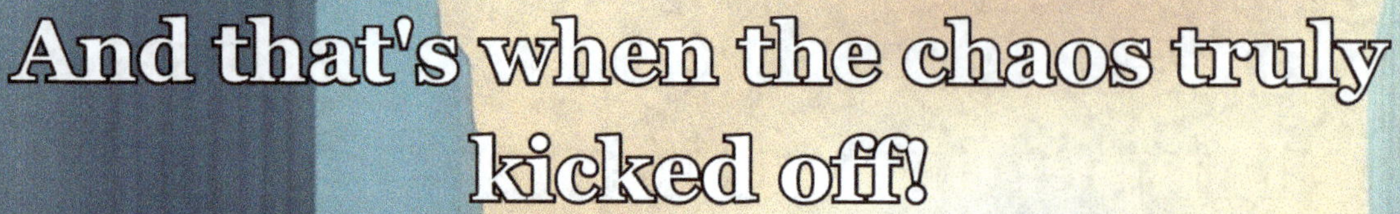

And that's when the chaos truly kicked off!

Hulking henchmen of all shapes and sizes swarmed the streets of every city in the U.S. They had even taken over every news outlet.

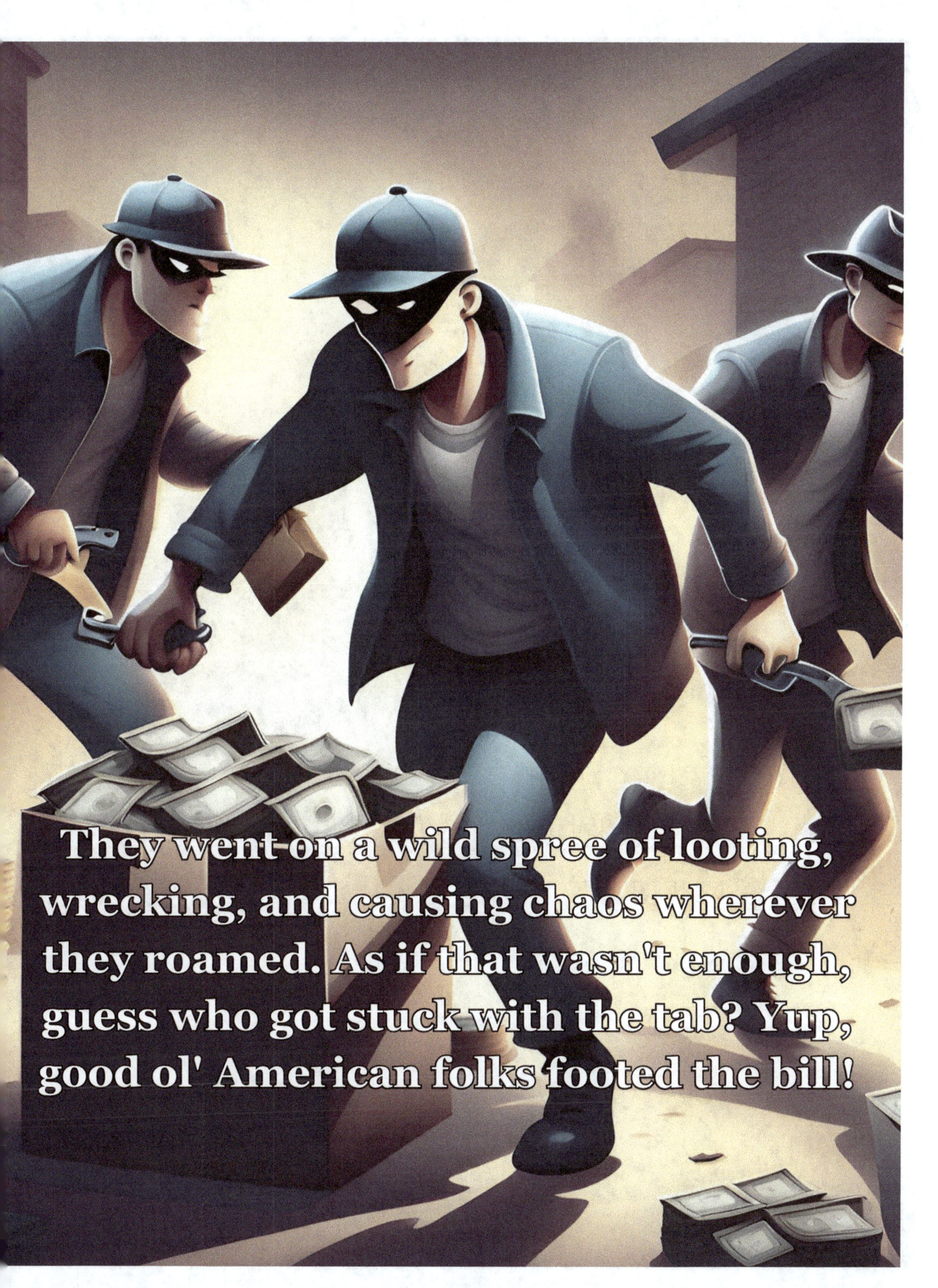
They went on a wild spree of looting, wrecking, and causing chaos wherever they roamed. As if that wasn't enough, guess who got stuck with the tab? Yup, good ol' American folks footed the bill!

The wicked Emperor Bidifer went all out, dispatching his money maestro to sneakily bump up prices in every corner grocery store.

The Evil Emperior Bidifer took out his relentless wrath on American babies. Vowing that millions of them would never take their first breath.

America's citizens sprinted in horror
at the glimpse of this wicked face.

Their flickering ember of hope dimmed, casting shadows upon their desperate souls. Nowhere remained sacred to seek refuge. There was no path left to tread in this hour of terror.

When suddenly, from afar, a lone superhero appeared.

It was M.T.G.

With her she brought no weapons of war or mass destruction. Just a whisper in the silence. And within that whisper, she wove her song...

"God Bless America, Land That I Love!"

Suddenly, the ground behind her was swarmed by the spirits of America's patriots. The echoes of freedom reverberated across the nation as they belted out the patriotic anthem.

When Lord Ackmith, Braggor, and Inaf caught wind of this anthem and witnessed the spirit of America's freedom, they fell to their knees and waved the white flag to surrender.

As the crowd watched the handover of Lord Ackmith, Inaf, and Braggor to the authorities, they quickly rallied behind M. T. G. and her quest to restore our beloved President Trump to his office.

The chorus of many swiftly merged into a single powerful voice, demanding the freedom of their adored President.

They found their dear President in a cave beneath the Georgia courthouse. M. T. G. leaned in and whispered, " Mr. President... Your country needs you!"

Filled with a patriotic zest for life, liberty, and the pursuit of happiness for all Americans, the President morphed into the legendary M.A.G.A. Trump!

With one fierce swoop, M.A.G.A. Trump permanently blinded the scale of justice.
Ensuring that the blindfold would never again be removed.

He shattered the veil of deceit cloaking the voting system, safeguarding it against any foreign or domestic meddling for all eternity.

The American economy made a grand comeback, allowing folks to shop for groceries like never before, with shelves stocked full of regular-sized goodies.

M. A. G. A. Trump crushed Emperor
Bidifers' obsession with electric cars,
bringing down gasoline prices with it.
America's drill-happy days were back, no
longer relying on fuel shipments from afar

Our tiny, yet-to-be-born citizens were shielded from harm once more.

Finally, MAGA Trump wrapped up his grand wall project. America's southern border was now as snug as a bug in a rug. Time for the citizens to kick back and relax! They would no longer have to worry about who was lurking in their backyards.

Our country's folks were over joyed!
Every shade, every background, all came
rushing in as President Trump made a
grand return to the White House.

The American people, in a resolute act, stripped Emperor Bidifer of all dominion. Swiftly, his alliance with Evil Emerita and The Shape Schiffter, was no more. Their grand scheme of world domination crumbled to dust.

Emperor Bidifer's sidekicks, Lord Ackmith, Inaf, and Braggor, got slapped with prison time for their mischief. On the bright side, they did get to munch on three squares a day - a unique combo of diet coke and meatloaf.

And just like that, the power was returned to the people - a government of the people, by the people, and for the people. Liberty was back where it belongs!

God Bless
America!
Land That I Love!